Patterning Techniques

Doodling and patterning are wonderful ways to embellish your images to make them unique to you and really stand out! You can add doodles to a design before coloring or after. Adding doodles after coloring works best on designs colored with markers, as described below.

Before Coloring

1 Start with a blank design.

2 Add little doodles like lines, circles, and other shapes. Patterns are just simple shapes that are repeated!

3 Color the design.

After Coloring

1 After coloring a design with markers, add details using fine-tip pens.

2 Add more details using gel pens (I used glitter gel pens here).

3 Add a final layer of detail using paint pens.

Tips
- Try adding details with pens, gel pens, paint pens, fine-tip markers, colored pencils, and anything else you can think of!
- Try layering different media on top of one other to see what effects you can create.

Shading

Shading is a great way to add depth and sophistication to a drawing. Even layering just one color on top of another color can be enough to indicate shading. And of course, you can combine different media to create shading. Here are two techniques to try!

Shading by Outlining

If you've never tried shading before, start with this easy outlining technique to help make your images pop! In this example, markers were used for both the base colors and the outlines, but you could also create the outlines with pens, gel pens, or colored pencils.

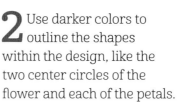

1 Color the design.

2 Use darker colors to outline the shapes within the design, like the two center circles of the flower and each of the petals.

3 For a little extra pizzazz, add dots!

Shading Colored Pencils on Top of Markers

1 Color your image with markers.

2 Use darker shades of your base colors in colored pencil to add shading. Here I used orange pencil to shade the yellow marker.

3 I used magenta and violet pencils to add shading to the pink marker areas.

Blending

Blending allows you to make smooth transitions between different tints and shades of a color when shading, and even between two different colors when creating gradients. Here are some simple techniques to produce flawless blends.

Alcohol-Based Markers

Alcohol-based markers can create smooth blends that have a painted look. You only need two colors to create a blend, but in this example I've used three shades of the same color: a light, a dark, and a color in between.

Tips

- It's easiest to create smooth transitions while your base layer is still damp.
- Don't be afraid to really work the marker into the paper—alcohol-based markers won't tear or pill the paper.
- Put a sheet or two of scrap paper underneath your coloring page to soak up any excess color that may seep through the paper.

1 Color your entire image with the lightest color. While this is still damp, use your middle color to add shading, focusing on the sides and bottom half of the shape.

2 Using your lightest color, go over the edges where the two colors meet to soften the transition.

3 Use your darkest color to add deeper shadows, focusing on the very outer edges and bottom of the shape.

4 Use your middle color to soften the edges between the dark and middle colors. If needed, use your light color on top of everything to smooth the transitions even more.

All of the colors in this flower were blended. Note the transitions from yellow to orange, from light pink to magenta, and from light blue to medium blue.

4 I used a dark blue pencil to shade the light blue marker areas. You can also use a white pencil to add details on top of the marker, as I did in the flower's center.

Tips

- When using colored pencils, apply more pressure to the areas that you want to appear darker.
- Use light-colored pencils on top of dark areas to create highlights.

Colored Pencils

In this example I've used three shades of each color: a light, a dark, and a color in between.

1 Color the design with your lightest colors. Then, lightly apply your middle colors over the areas that you want to appear darker.

2 Lightly apply your dark colors where you want the deepest shadows. Apply more pressure where you want the color to be the strongest.

3 Use your middle colors to go over the area where the middle and dark colors overlap. Apply pressure as necessary to smooth the transitions.

4 Use your lightest colors to go over the areas where the light and middle colors overlap, applying pressure as needed.

Tips

- Applying a colored pencil in a circular motion makes the color appear more seamless than if you use back-and-forth strokes.
- Always use light pressure at first, and apply more pressure as you add more layers.
- A slightly blunt colored pencil works better for this technique than one with a super sharp point.

Colored Pencils with a Blender Pencil

1 Lightly apply color using small overlapping circles (as opposed to back-and-forth strokes). Leave areas completely white where you would like to create highlights.

2 Using the same colored pencil and the circular motion, go back and add a second layer of color, applying more pressure to the areas that you want to appear darker.

Colored Pencils with Baby Oil

1 Color the darkest areas first.

2 Next, color in the lighter areas.

3 Dip a cotton swab or tortillon (paper blending stump) into baby oil. Blot the excess on a paper towel. Gently rub the swab over the colored areas. Use a different swab for each color group. After the baby oil has dried, you can add more color if needed and use more baby oil to blend it.

3 Go over everything with a blender pencil, using it the same way you would use a colored pencil. The blender will smooth your colored pencil marks and increase the intensity of the color.

4 You can create additional shading using a darker color, as I've done at the end of each petal. Repeat these steps with different colors for the rest of your design.

Color Theory

One of the most common questions beginners ask when they're getting ready to color is "What colors should I use?" The fun thing about coloring is that there is no such thing as right or wrong. You can use whatever colors you want, wherever you want! Coloring offers a lot of freedom, allowing you to explore a whole world of possibilities.

With that said, if you're looking for a little guidance, it is helpful to understand some basic color theory. Let's look at the nifty color wheel in the shape of a flower below. Each color is labeled with a P, S, or T, which stands for Primary, Secondary, and Tertiary.

Working toward the center of the six large primary and secondary color petals, you'll see three rows of lighter colors, which are called tints. A **tint** is a color plus white. Moving in from the tints, you'll see three rows of darker colors, which are called shades. A **shade** is a color plus black. The colors on the top half of the color wheel are considered **warm** colors (red, yellow, orange), and the colors on the bottom half of the color wheel are considered **cool** colors (green, blue, purple). Colors opposite one another on the color wheel are called **complementary**, and colors that are next to each other are called **analogous**.

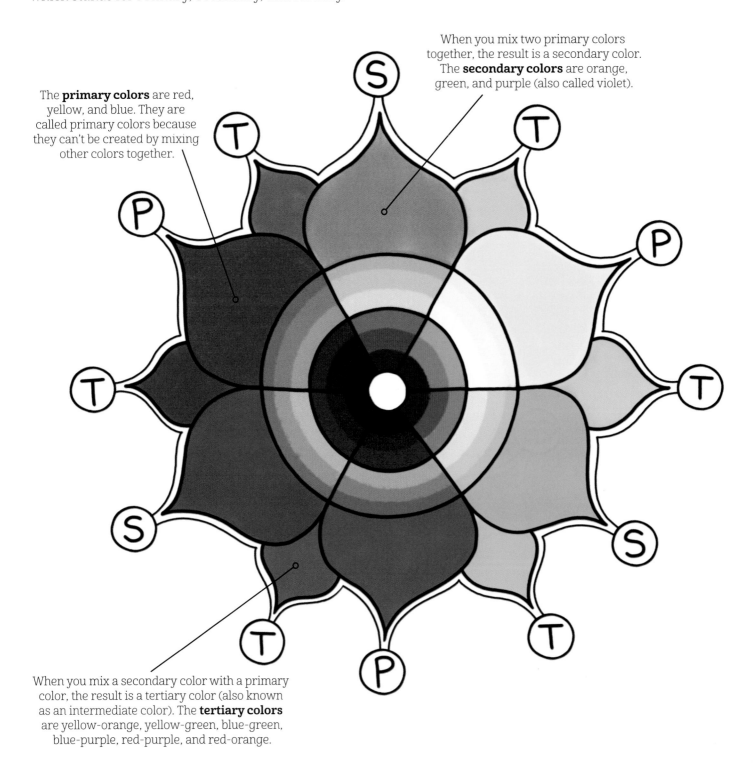

The **primary colors** are red, yellow, and blue. They are called primary colors because they can't be created by mixing other colors together.

When you mix two primary colors together, the result is a secondary color. The **secondary colors** are orange, green, and purple (also called violet).

When you mix a secondary color with a primary color, the result is a tertiary color (also known as an intermediate color). The **tertiary colors** are yellow-orange, yellow-green, blue-green, blue-purple, red-purple, and red-orange.

Color Combinations

There are so many ways to combine colors that sometimes it can be overwhelming to think of the possibilities...but it can also be a ton of fun deciding what color scheme you are going to use!

It's important to remember that there is no right or wrong way to color a piece of art, because everyone's tastes are different when it comes to color. Each of us naturally gravitates toward certain colors or color schemes, so over time, you'll learn which colors you tend to use the most (you might already have an idea!). Color theory can help you understand how colors relate to each other, and perhaps open your eyes to new color combos you might not have tried before!

Check out the butterflies below. They are colored in many different ways, using some of the color combinations mentioned in the color wheel section before. Note how each color combo affects the overall appearance and "feel" of the butterfly. As you look at these butterflies, ask yourself which ones you are most attracted to and why. Which color combinations feel more dynamic to you? Which ones pop out and grab you? Which ones seem to blend harmoniously? Do any combinations seem rather dull to you? By asking yourself these questions, you can gain an understanding of the color schemes you prefer.

Tip

Now you're ready to start experimenting on paper. When you're getting ready to color a piece of art, test various color combos on scrap paper or in a sketchbook to get a feel for the way the colors work together. When you color, remember to also use the white of the paper as a "color." Not every portion of the art piece has to be filled in with color. Often, leaving a bit of white here and there adds some wonderful variety to the image!

Warm colors

Cool colors

Warm colors with cool accents

Cool colors with warm accents

Tints and shades of red

Tints and shades of blue

Analogous colors

Complementary colors

Split complementary colors

 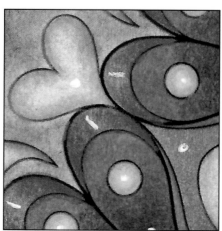 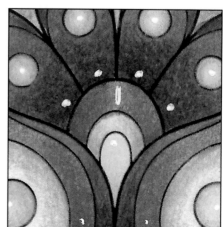

© Thaneeya McArdle, *www.thaneeya.com*. From *Power of Love Coloring Book* © Design Originals, *www.D-Originals.com*

always & forever

My heart is, and always will be, yours.

—Jane Austen, *Sense and Sensibility*

_____
_____
_____
_____
_____
_____
_____
_____
_____

Always and Forever

When you realize you want to spend the rest
of your life with somebody, you want the rest of
your life to start as soon as possible.

—When Harry Met Sally

_____
_____
_____
_____
_____
_____
_____
_____
_____

I Love You

A joyful heart is the inevitable result
of a heart burning with love.

—Mother Teresa

_____
_____
_____
_____
_____
_____
_____
_____
_____
_____

Swirly Heart

Love is the greatest refreshment in life.

—Pablo Picasso

_____
_____
_____
_____
_____
_____
_____
_____
_____
_____

Sloth Love

Love is, above all, the gift of oneself.

—Jean Anouilh

_____

_____

_____

_____

_____

_____

_____

_____

_____

_____

Owl Hug

LOVE CONQUERS hate

I have decided to stick to love. . . .
Hate is too great a burden to bear.

—Martin Luther King, Jr.

_____

_____

_____

_____

_____

_____

_____

_____

_____

Love Conquers Hate

Love is like a friendship caught on fire.

—Bruce Lee

Sharing Music

Never love anyone who treats you
like you're ordinary.

—Oscar Wilde

_____
_____
_____
_____
_____
_____
_____
_____
_____

Love What Makes You Unique

With your best shading work, lean deep into the petals,
making them look super sniffable!

A friend is someone who knows all about you
and still loves you.

—Elbert Hubbard

_____

_____

_____

_____

_____

_____

_____

_____

_____

Lovesong

© Thaneeya McArdle, *www.thaneeya.com*. From *Power of Love Coloring Book* © Design Originals, *www.D-Originals.com*

Mediums matter! The artist here uses high-quality alcohol markers to layer on the soft red pelts of these otters.

Two lives, two hearts, joined together in friendship,
united forever in love.

—Unknown

Otter Couple

Lettering never has to be boring—look at the gradient of warm colors used to warm up the word "Love"!

Love liberates. It doesn't bind.

—Maya Angelou

_____
_____
_____
_____
_____
_____
_____
_____
_____

Love is Love

© Thaneeya McArdle, *www.thaneeya.com.* From *Power of Love Coloring Book* © Design Originals, *www.D-Originals.com*

When you want to take a coloring to the next level, the white gel pen is your best friend! Dot to your heart's content!

Nobody has ever measured, even poets,
how much a heart can hold.

—Zelda Fitzgerald

Scroll Heart

Even a minimal number of colors, used well,
can be breathtaking in a coloring.

Love makes your soul crawl out
from its hiding place.

—Zora Neale Hurston

_____

_____

_____

_____

_____

_____

_____

_____

_____

_____

Heart Mandala

© Thaneeya McArdle, *www.thaneeya.com*. From *Power of Love Coloring Book* © Design Originals, *www.D-Originals.com*

Feel free to take advantage of the suggested patterns to color in the kitties, but don't be afraid to design your own cat!

Whatever our souls are made of,
his and mine are the same.

—Emily Brontë

Kitty Couple

With pleasant hues of pink, red, yellow, orange, blue, and green, you can pair together all kinds of interesting contrasts that will keep the eye moving around your picture.

The supreme happiness in life is the conviction
that we are loved—loved for ourselves,
or rather, loved in spite of ourselves.

—Victor Hugo

_____
_____
_____
_____
_____
_____
_____
_____

Giant Heart

Here you have the panorama of human skin tones to play with.
Variety is the spice of life!

You never lose by loving.
You always lose by holding back.

—Barbara de Angelis

_____
_____
_____
_____
_____
_____
_____
_____
_____
_____
_____

United by Love

If I had a flower for every time I thought of you . . .
I could walk through my garden forever.

—Claudia Adrienne Grandi

Sharing is Caring

This hand sign is a simple but profound gesture in American Sign Language that means "I love you."

I Love You Sign

You know you're in love when
you can't fall asleep because reality is
finally better than your dreams.

—Unknown

_____

_____

_____

_____

_____

_____

_____

_____

_____

Bunny Love

We are most alive when we're in love.

—John Updike

_____

_____

_____

_____

_____

_____

_____

_____

_____

Love is in the Air

I carry your heart (I carry it in my heart).

—e.e. cummings

_____
_____
_____
_____
_____
_____
_____
_____
_____
_____

Sacred Heart

English: **love**

French: **amour**

Spanish: **amor**

Icelandic: **ást**

Russian: любовь

Arabic: الحبّ

Hindi: मोहब्बत

Chinese (Simplified): 爱

Japanese: 愛

Thai: ความรัก

Swahili: **upendo**

Hebrew: אהבה

Love Languages

If you would be loved, love, and be loveable.

—Benjamin Franklin

_____
_____
_____
_____
_____
_____
_____
_____

I Love Myself

Fortune and love favor the brave.

—Latin proverb

_____

_____

_____

_____

_____

_____

_____

_____

_____

_____

Hamsa Heart

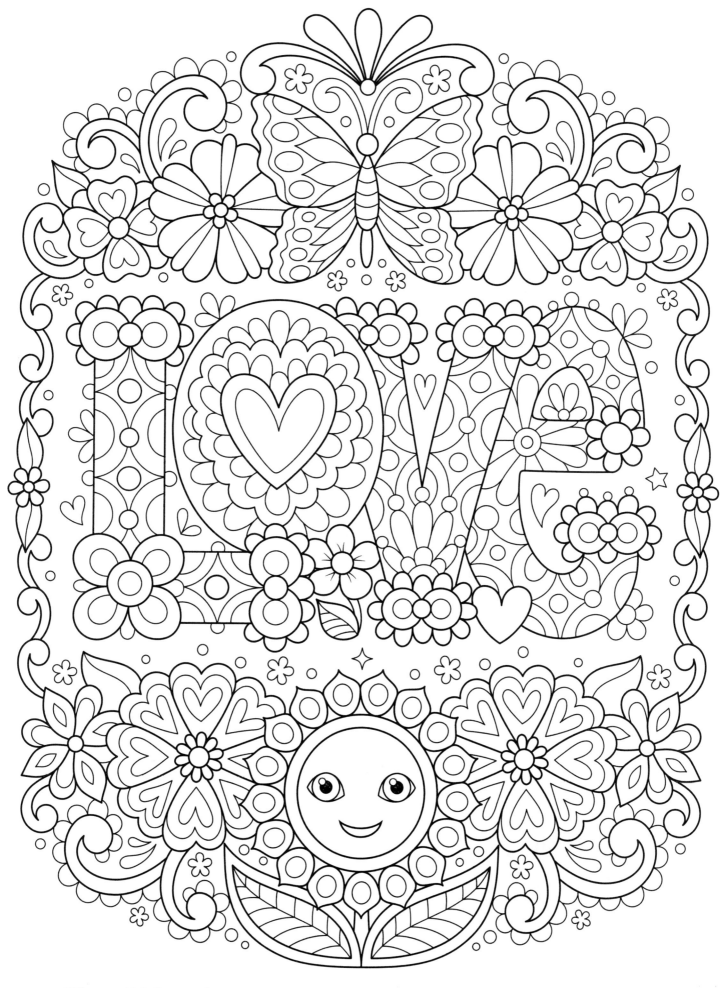

Less is more unless it's love.

—Ben Mittleman

_____
_____
_____
_____
_____
_____
_____
_____
_____
_____

Just Love

Climb aboard the Love Train

The past is behind us,
love is in front and all around us.

—Terri Guillemets

_____
_____
_____
_____
_____
_____
_____
_____
_____

Love Train

The most important thing in life is to learn how
to give out love, and to let it come in.

—Morrie Schwartz

_____
_____
_____
_____
_____
_____
_____
_____
_____

Limitless Love

A kiss is a lovely trick designed by nature to stop speech when words become superfluous.

—Unknown

_____
_____
_____
_____
_____
_____
_____
_____
_____
_____
_____

Rainbows

I love you not only for what you are,
but for what I am when I am with you.

—Roy Croft

_____
_____
_____
_____
_____
_____
_____
_____
_____
_____

Home

Love is patient, love is kind. It does not envy,
it does not boast, it is not proud. It does not dishonor
others, it is not self-seeking, it is not easily angered,
it keeps no record of wrongs. Love does not delight in
evil but rejoices with the truth. It always protects,
always trusts, always hopes, always perseveres.
Love never fails.

—1 Corinthians 13:4-8

Sun Love

A hundred hearts would be too few
To carry all my love for you.

—Unknown

_____
_____
_____
_____
_____
_____
_____
_____
_____
_____
_____

You're Amazing

Your heart is free.
Have the courage to follow it.

—Braveheart

_____
_____
_____
_____
_____
_____
_____
_____
_____
_____

Love Hands